SPY GUIDE

CYBER SPYING

ELSIE OLSON

Abdo & Daughters
MIDDLE GRADE NONFICTION

An imprint of Abdo Publishing
abdobooks.com

ABDOBOOKS.COM

Published by Abdo Publishing, a division of ABDO, PO Box 398166, Minneapolis, Minnesota 55439. Copyright © 2025 by Abdo Consulting Group, Inc. International copyrights reserved in all countries. No part of this book may be reproduced in any form without written permission from the publisher. Abdo & Daughters™ is a trademark and logo of Abdo Publishing.

Printed in the United States of America, North Mankato, Minnesota
052024
092024

Design: Kelly Doudna, Mighty Media, Inc.
Production: Mighty Media, Inc.
Editor: Katherine Chu
Cover Photographs: Adobe Stock, iStockphoto

Interior Photographs: Adobe Stock, pp. 1, 12, 27, 29 (bottom), 52, 53, 58 (bottom), 59; AP Images, pp. 36, 48, 61 (bottom middle); Flickr, pp. 4-5; iStockphoto, pp. 44, 49; Library of Congress, pp. 13, 15, 16; Shutterstock Images, pp. 8, 24, 26, 28, 29 (top), 32, 34, 37, 38, 39, 40, 42-43, 45, 50-51, 54, 56, 58 (top), 61 (top left, top right, bottom left, bottom right); Wikimedia Commons, pp. 7, 10-11, 14, 17, 19, 20, 21, 22-23, 25, 30-31, 33, 47, 60

Design Elements: Adobe Stock

Library of Congress Control Number: 2023949479

Publisher's Cataloging-in-Publication Data
Names: Olson, Elsie, author.
Title: Cyber spying / by Elsie Olson
Description: Minneapolis, Minnesota : Abdo Publishing, 2025 | Series: Spy guide | Includes online resources and index.
Identifiers: ISBN 9781098293130 (lib. bdg.) | ISBN 9798384912408 (ebook)
Subjects: LCSH: Security systems--Juvenile literature. | World Wide Web--Security measures--Juvenile literature. | Computer crimes--United States--Prevention--Juvenile literature. | Internet in espionage--Juvenile literature. | Espionage--Juvenile literature. | Spies--Juvenile literature.
Classification: DDC 327.12--dc23

CONTENTS

Secrets Unleashed 5

A History of Hacking 11

Cyber Spying 101 23

Threat Actors and Techniques 31

Social Engineering and Cyber Sabotage 43

Spying into the Future 51

So You Want to Be a Cyber Defender? 58

Timeline 60

Glossary 62

Online Resources 63

Index 64

The intelligence that Chelsea Manning (*pictured*) gave to WikiLeaks is believed to be the biggest unauthorized release of secret information in US history.

CHAPTER 1

SECRETS UNLEASHED

It's a humid summer evening in 2010, but US president Barack Obama is keeping his cool. Standing in front of a team of reporters in the White House Rose Garden, he addresses a recent government scandal. Since April, the website WikiLeaks has leaked, or published without consent, thousands of classified documents related to the US wars in Iraq and Afghanistan. The documents cover a period from 2004 to 2009.

President Obama presents an image of calm. He says that while he is concerned about the leaks, he does not feel the documents reveal much new information. But behind the scenes, members of President Obama's administration are panicking. The leaks have threatened the identities of US spies overseas. The documents have also revealed information about US military operations and practices that could be useful to the country's enemies. Some leaks have caused

THE ONION ROUTER

WikiLeaks relied on an online browser called the Onion Router (TOR) to protect the identities of its sources and keep its secrets flowing. TOR allows a user to keep their online activities anonymous. Normally, internet service providers (ISPs) can track everything a person does on the internet. The ISP can share this information with a third party, such as advertisers or governments. TOR works by sending internet traffic through a series of random servers, making it nearly impossible to track the person using the tool.

public outrage. One top-secret video shows a US military helicopter mistakenly firing on a group of civilians and journalists in Iraq. The video has caused some people to question the actions of the US military.

AN ARREST

That May, the US military arrested US Army intelligence analyst Bradley Manning, later known as Chelsea Manning, for leaking the video and classified documents. But WikiLeaks wasn't done. By the end of 2010, the website had published more than 500,000 classified documents. These included 250,000 sensitive communications between diplomats as well as additional military documents.

HERO OR TRAITOR?

WikiLeaks had been known for publishing classified information since its formation in 2006. But the 2010 leaks brought international attention to the platform. Leaders around the world condemned the leaks and US politicians were furious. Much of this anger was directed at one man: Australian computer programmer and WikiLeaks founder Julian Assange.

Assange is a talented hacker. As a teenager, he broke into the computer networks of several government agencies.

Assange had always been a divisive figure. He described himself as an information activist and believed information should be accessible to everyone. Assange founded WikiLeaks as a platform for something he called scientific journalism. He saw WikiLeaks as a place where people could access primary sources directly with limited opinions or comments from traditional journalists.

People had mixed feelings about Assange after the leaks. Many considered him to be a journalist who was simply reporting the

Assange's supporters protest his imprisonment and possible extradition to the US.

truth. His supporters hailed Assange as a hero who was protecting their right to information and free speech. Others felt he had violated the privacy of individuals and threatened national security. Assange faced arrest and criminal charges from countries around the world. To avoid arrest, he applied for asylum at the Ecuadorian embassy in London, England. The embassy granted his request, allowing Assange to stay there.

ANOTHER LEAK

Though Manning was in prison and Assange was at the Ecuadorian embassy, WikiLeaks continued to publish. It had no shortage of sources. In 2016, the website published a series of emails related to the campaign of US presidential candidate Hillary Clinton. The emails seemed to show that the Democratic National Committee (DNC) had helped Clinton win the presidential nomination over her main Democratic rival, Bernie Sanders. Some experts believed these emails and the public disagreement surrounding them contributed to Clinton losing the election to Republican candidate Donald Trump.

AN UNCERTAIN FATE

In April 2019, Ecuador took back its offer of asylum to Assange due to his multiple violations of international law and breaking his asylum agreement. British authorities finally arrested Assange, and soon after, the US Department of Justice charged him with violating the US Espionage Act for the 2010 leaks. Assange was sent to Belmarsh Prison in London while British leaders debated whether to hand him over to the US. In the meantime, WikiLeaks kept publishing classified information. As of 2023, Assange was still imprisoned, waiting to learn his fate.

THE ESPIONAGE ACT OF 1917

Both Manning and Assange were charged under the Espionage Act of 1917. The US enacted this law shortly after entering World War I. It prohibited anyone from stealing, copying, photographing, or recording information related to national defense with the intent to harm the US. People who violated the act could face fines, prison, or even execution if the espionage crime was considered serious enough.

Sun Tzu's *The Art of War* is one of the first books to document different military strategies.

CHAPTER 2

A HISTORY OF HACKING

THE 2010 WIKILEAKS CASE IS ONE OF THE BEST-KNOWN examples of cyber espionage. This is the practice of using technology to access secret information or intelligence, such as military or political secrets. This information can help government or military organizations learn about their rivals, assess possible threats, sabotage their enemies, and even prevent possible attacks. Many countries secretly pay hacker groups to spy on their behalf. And these cyber spies can influence world events in a way spies of the past could only dream of.

EARLY ESPIONAGE

Espionage has a history almost as old as civilization itself. Chinese general and military strategist Sun Tzu is credited with outlining the importance of espionage more than 2,500 years ago in his book *The Art of War*. The book states,

THE BLACK CHAMBER

Cabinet noir is French for "black chamber." Many European countries had these secret spy chambers in post offices. Spies there would carefully open letters being sent to foreign countries. They would copy the letters and reseal the originals. The original letters were then sent to their intended destinations. Meanwhile, spies worked to crack any codes in the copied letters, selling the intelligence they gathered.

"Foreknowledge cannot be gotten from ghosts and spirits, cannot be had by analogy, cannot be found out by calculation. It must be obtained from people, people who know the conditions of the enemy." This means that the best, most sound knowledge can only come from the work of skilled spies.

For thousands of years, human eyes and ears were the only way to reliably access intelligence. Spies might be servants who worked for political or military leaders. And sometimes agents spying for one country agreed to spy for another, becoming double agents. In the 1600s, France's King Louis XIV employed agents throughout Europe to read private letters and report back to him. This intelligence system became known as a *cabinet noir*.

Sun Tzu

REAL-TIME TALK

For most of history, spying was slow work. It sometimes took weeks to pass intelligence from a spy to decision-makers. That all changed with the rise of electronic communication. In 1837, Samuel F.B. Morse invented the first form of electronic communication, the telegraph. Morse developed a code based on a system of dots and dashes that represented letters and numbers. A transmitter sent the dots and dashes, in the form of short and long electric pulses, through a wire from one telegraph station to a receiver at another station. There, a telegraph operator decoded the message.

Samuel F.B. Morse

By 1861, telegraph wires stretched across the US, allowing people, including government and military leaders, to communicate across long distances with one another instantly. US president and Union leader Abraham Lincoln relied heavily on the technology to communicate during the American Civil War.

The telegraph also opened the door for the first generation of cyber spies. For the first time, leaders could use technology to gain access to intelligence. During the Civil War, Lincoln authorized

Morse came up with the idea for the telegraph in 1832 after learning about the newly discovered electromagnet. Experts think he made his first working telegraph model around 1835.

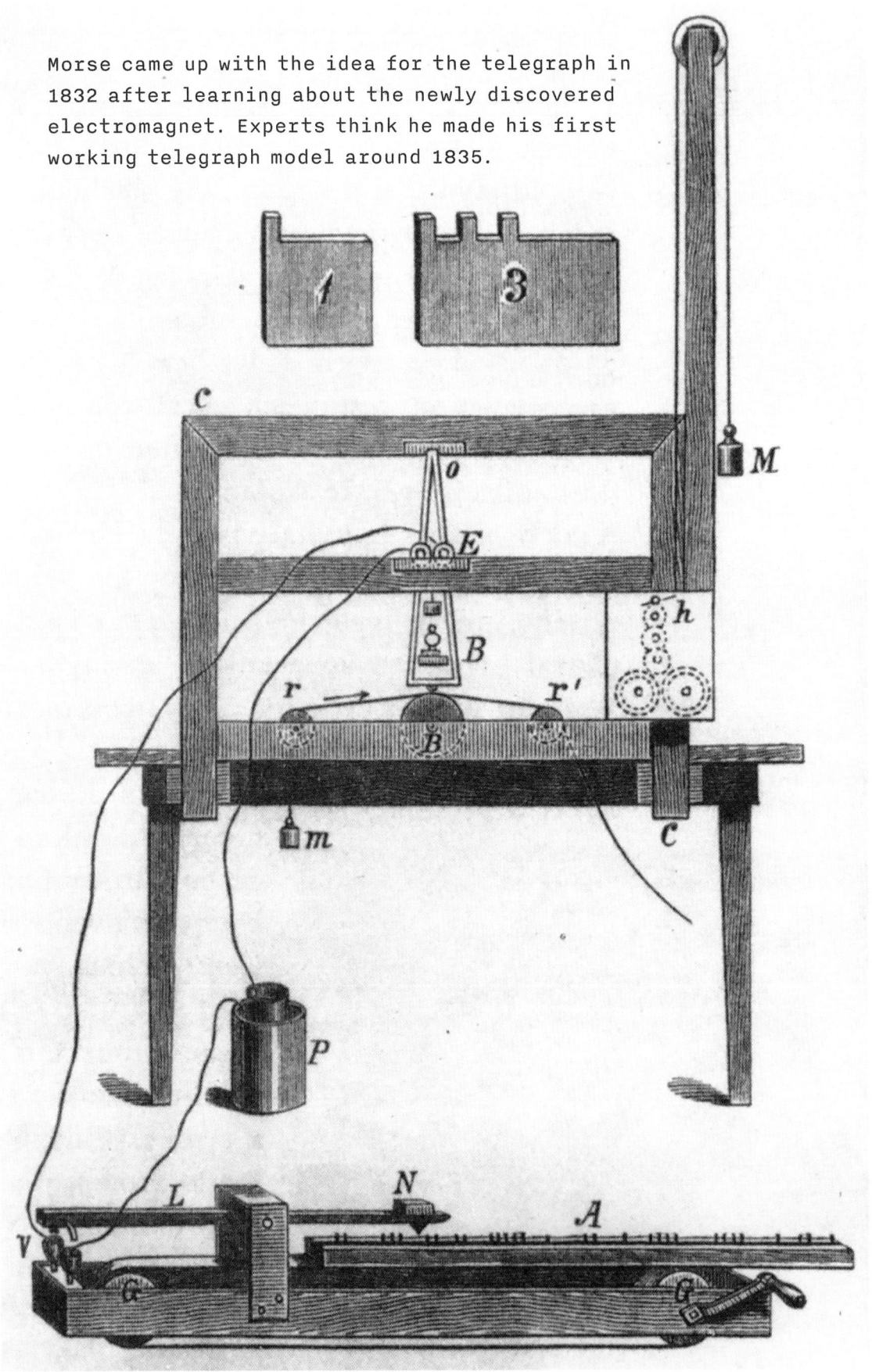

his secretary of war, Edwin Stanton, to read all telegrams. These included dispatches from journalists, government workers, and private citizens. Both Union and Confederate spies were also known to eavesdrop on telegraph conversations using a technique called tapping the wire. A spy would attach a device that could detect electrical pulses traveling through the wire. The device could not only intercept telegraph messages but also send false messages.

THE RISE OF WIRELESS

By the time World War I broke out in 1914, the telegraph had been largely replaced by wireless communication, which was more

Many navies and air forces used wireless radio communication during both World War I and World War II.

In 1909, Marconi received a Nobel Prize for his work with wireless communication.

reliable. In 1894, Italian inventor Guglielmo Marconi developed a wireless communication system that could send messages using a type of electromagnetic radiation known as radio waves. These waves of energy carried electronic signals through the air. Marconi built devices called radios that used these waves to send messages wirelessly.

Wireless communication offered huge advantages over telegraph communication. It was highly mobile and didn't rely on lines and stations. During World War I and World War II, wireless operators could also send and receive messages from anywhere using only a transmitter and a receiver. But wireless communication had a major drawback for intelligence agencies. Anyone could intercept wireless signals by listening to the same frequency. That meant the enemy could hear any wartime messages. To protect their secrets, the military had to encrypt their messages.

COLD WAR COMPUTERS

After World War II ended in 1945, the US transitioned into another conflict, the Cold War. It lasted from 1947 to 1991. During this period, the US and its allies competed against the Union of Soviet Socialist Republics (USSR) and its allies for technological and military

THE HISTORY OF THE COMPUTER

During World War II, a pair of US engineers invented the first electronic programmable computer, the Electronic Numerical Integrator and Computer (ENIAC), in 1946. Its first assignment was performing calculations for the construction of a hydrogen bomb. Although it had limited capabilities, especially compared to later computers, ENIAC was the most powerful machine of its time. It was also enormous. At 50 by 30 feet (15 by 9 m), it took up an entire room!

Wires plugged into boards called plugboards communicated calculation instructions to ENIAC. It could take scientists days to set up the plugboards for each new calculation.

superiority. During this time, these countries never openly fought one another. Instead, they waged secret battles using information to keep their rivals from becoming too powerful. Throughout the Cold War, the capabilities of computers increased as well. With the rise of the computer came a new generation of spies known as cyber spies.

During the Cold War, intelligence agencies used computers to decode messages and analyze intelligence. Computers monitored and intercepted electronic communications, such as telephone calls and radio signals. Multiple computers in one location could communicate with one another using wired connections on private networks. But the only way to transfer digital information to and from computers in different locations was to download it onto a computer disc. But the discs could be lost or intercepted. So, the US government sought a way to transfer information between computers without using discs.

ARPANET

In the 1960s, the US Department of Defense (DOD) set up a system called ARPANET. This system allowed computers in different locations to communicate on the same network by sending digital information through telephone lines. The DOD hoped this would allow government researchers to share information with one another safely and securely.

On October 29, 1969, ARPANET delivered its first message. The message, a single word, was sent from Los Angeles, California, to Stanford, California. Only two letters of the message came through

The logbook entry of the first message sent using ARPANET. The message was the word *login*. But only the letters *l* and *o* were transmitted before the system crashed.

before the computers crashed, but it was considered the first successful internet message.

THE INTERNET IS BORN

ARPANET continued to expand throughout the 1970s, but it was only available to government contractors. Similar networks were created for other government agencies and universities, but the different networks could not connect to one another. So, computer scientists began developing a standard protocol for communication, which would allow different computers on different networks to communicate with each other across long distances.

The world's first website was created by Berners-Lee and hosted on his computer (*pictured*). The website explained how the World Wide Web worked.

On January 1, 1983, ARPANET officially adopted the Transfer Control Protocol/Internetwork Protocol. Experts consider this date to be the birth of the modern internet. The protocol became the new standard for internet communication, and other networks soon adopted it.

THE WORLD WIDE WEB

The 1980s and 1990s also saw a rise in demand for personal computers. These small but powerful machines were affordable and accessible enough to be used in homes, schools, and businesses.

In 1989, computer scientist Tim Berners-Lee invented the World Wide Web (WWW). This was a worldwide system of connected web pages and documents that people could access through the internet. Thanks to the WWW, people could find, access, and create an enormous amount of content.

The WWW was a huge success, especially as more people gained access to the internet. By 2000, there were more than 10,000 ISPs and nearly 400 million WWW users. The internet connected people from all over the world, creating communities and giving people access to more content than ever before. But it also created a brand-new world for cyber spies.

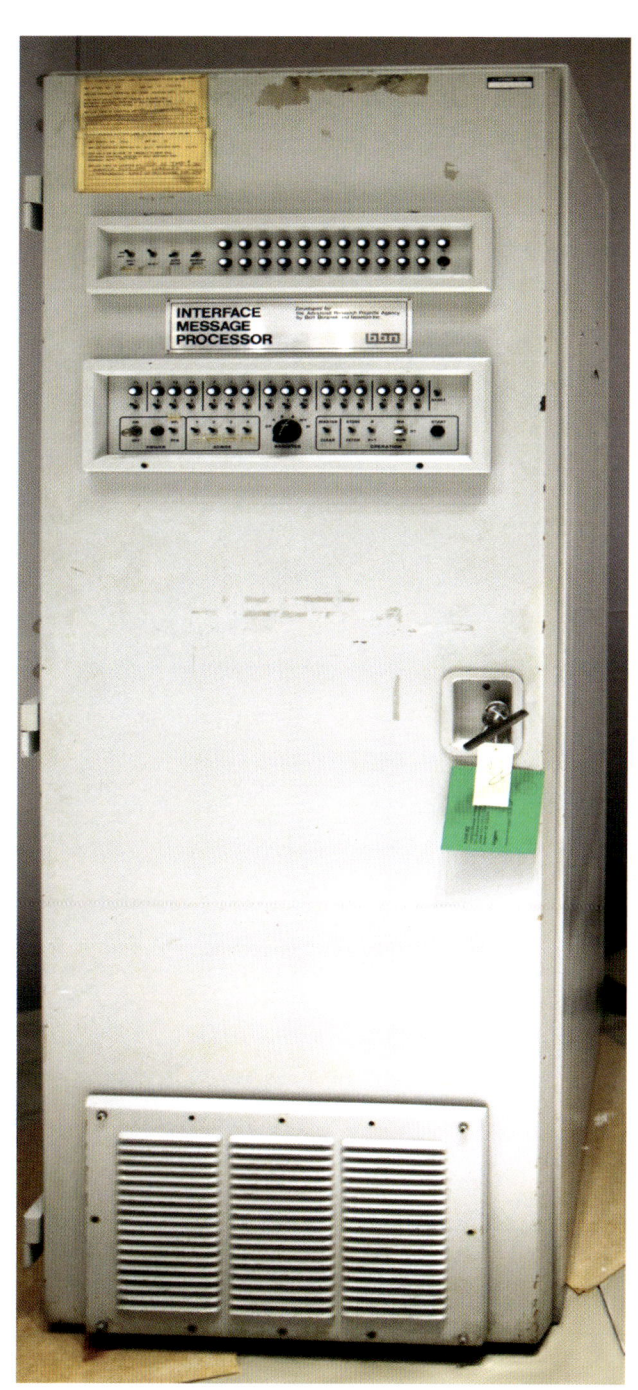

From the late 1960s to 1989, the Interface Message Processor connected the different networks using ARPANET. Many consider it to be the first router.

Computers that were affected by the unknown program slowed down so much that functions such as sending emails were delayed for days.

CHAPTER 3

CYBER SPYING 101

On November 2, 1988, a computer at the Massachusetts Institute of Technology (MIT) released a new program on the internet. The program exploited weaknesses in a network and gained access to other computers. Once inside a computer, it multiplied itself and exploited other computers on the network.

The program spread like wildfire. Within 24 hours, it had gained access to more than 6,000 computers, or 10 percent of all the internet-connected computers in existence. At the time, universities, research organizations, and government agencies such as NASA owned most of these computers.

Although the program didn't damage or delete computer files, it used an enormous amount of computing energy. As a result, computers around the globe slowed to a snail's pace. Some universities decided to wipe their systems, while others shut down their networks while they tried to find a fix.

THE FIRST HACKER

While computer programmers tried to fix the problem created by the program, others tried to find and punish whoever had launched it. A few days later, the *New York Times* published a story calling the program a "virus" and revealing its creator to be a 23-year-old student named Robert Tappan Morris.

At the time, Morris was studying computer science at Cornell University in Ithaca, New York. He had designed the program, later called the Morris Worm, to see if he could hack, or break into, computer networks without being detected. Morris hacked into an MIT computer to release his program. However, an error in his programming caused the virus to multiply out of control. Eventually, Morris was charged under the Computer Fraud and Abuse Act.

Morris became a professor at MIT (*pictured*) in 1999.

As punishment, he had to pay a fine and complete 400 hours of community service.

Morris also provided computer network managers with instructions for how to remove the program, limiting the overall damage. But the incident opened the world's eyes to the dangers of computer worms and viruses as well as the need

Morris was the first person convicted under the Computer Fraud and Abuse Act, which was passed in 1986.

WORM OR VIRUS?

The *New York Times* referred to Morris's program as a computer virus, but it was actually a computer worm. Like a biological virus, a computer virus must be attached to a host. This can be a document or file that is opened by a user on a computer, activating the virus. Once activated, the virus can copy itself and spread. A computer worm doesn't require a host file or any human interaction to activate. Instead, it gains access to a computer by exploiting a security vulnerability before it automatically multiplies and spreads.

for cybersecurity. Morris also inspired a new group of hackers. And it wasn't long before government and military intelligence agencies found ways to use hacking and cyber sabotage for their own benefit.

CYBER INTELLIGENCE

Modern cyber espionage and cybersecurity might be the most important aspects of intelligence gathering and counterespionage. The US has several intelligence organizations that work together to both openly and secretly gather intelligence and prevent espionage against the US.

The FBI Counterintelligence Program works to expose, prevent, and investigate intelligence activities in the US. It also works to protect US intelligence agency secrets.

Online identity thieves sometimes try to steal people's banking information. The thieves can use this information to take out loans or make unwanted purchases in a victim's name.

    The Federal Bureau of Investigation (FBI) is the primary US government agency charged with investigating and preventing cybercrimes, including cyber espionage. Officially, the US does not admit to engaging in cyber espionage. In fact, no country has an official cyber espionage operation. However, experts believe that many countries, including the US, secretly sponsor groups called threat actors to conduct cyber espionage on their behalf.

    A threat actor is any person or group who intentionally causes harm to another person, organization, or government using digital means. This might include secretly downloading classified military files or unleashing a computer virus that damages a company's servers. It could even mean stealing someone's identity online.

TOOLS OF THE TRADE: CYBER EDITION

Cyber spies use digital tools to steal information without detection. Explore some of the top tools and techniques used by cyber spies.

KEYLOGGER

Also called a keystroke logger, this software can record every single key typed on a computer.

TROJAN HORSE

A Trojan horse is a file or application that appears innocent but secretly contains malware, or malicious software. When a user opens or downloads the file or application, the malware is installed on their computer.

BOTNETS

Robot networks, also known as botnets, are networks of computers that are taken over by hackers. The hackers

The USSR created the first keylogger in the 1970s, using it to record the keystrokes on typewriters.

American biologist Joseph Popp developed the first known Trojan horse in 1989.

then use the networks for further espionage and cyberattacks. Hacker Khan Smith created the first botnet in 2000.

RANSOMWARE

Ransomware is a type of malware that encrypts all the files on a device, locking the computer user out until they pay the hacker a fee, or ransom.

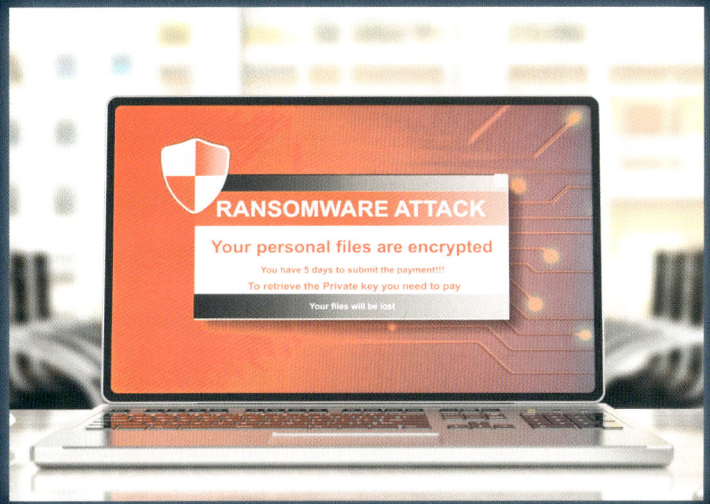

Popp launched a ransomware attack on attendees of a World Health Organization AIDS conference in 1989. It locked the attendees' computers until they paid ransom.

SPYWARE

Spyware is a type of software that tracks a user's computer activity, such as the websites they visit. Spyware can be used to steal private information, such as passwords, from a person's computer.

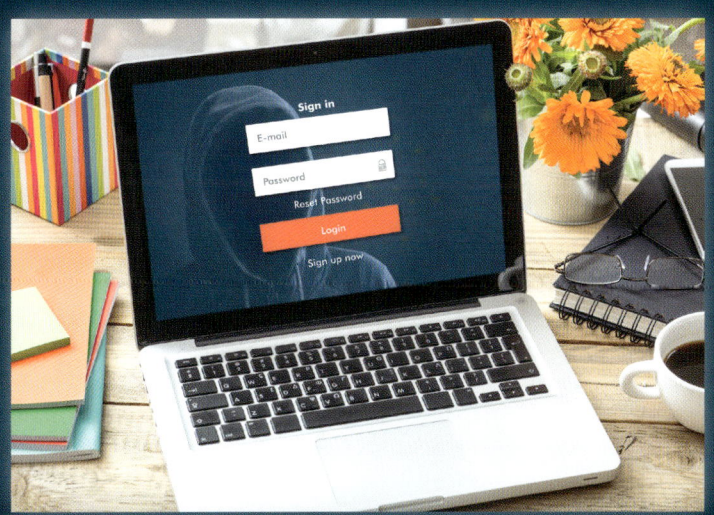

Online thieves often sell the information they gather from spyware.

Sandia National Laboratories was established in the 1940s. It became a US Department of Energy National Laboratory in 1979, developing technology to advance US national security.

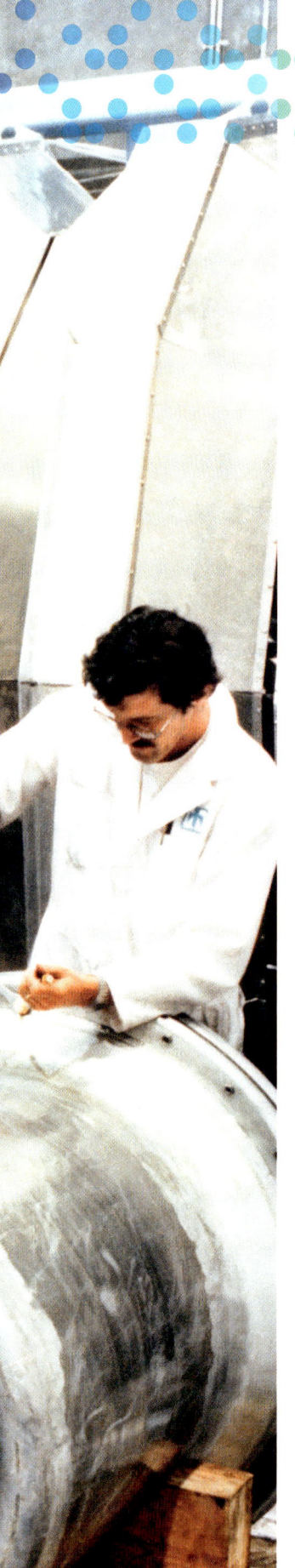

CHAPTER 4

THREAT ACTORS AND TECHNIQUES

After months spending his nights hunting spies online, Shawn Carpenter finally made a breakthrough. It was March 2004, and he worked for Sandia National Laboratories in Albuquerque, New Mexico, a research and development lab that worked for the US government. Since 2003, Carpenter had been investigating a series of cyberattacks on Sandia and other government agencies from his home in Albuquerque.

The swiftness and focus of the attacks impressed Carpenter. The hackers were in and out of each computer system in less than 30 minutes. Once inside, the hackers accessed the computer's hard drive, downloading as many files as they could. Then they would exit the system, leaving nothing behind except a silent beacon that allowed them to easily reenter the same system later. It was a brilliant technique, and one that very few hackers could pull off. In fact, the attacks were so similar, Carpenter was certain that they were executed by the same group of hackers.

TITAN RAIN

Carpenter had chased the hackers across the internet for the past few months. He followed them from computer to computer, tracing the attacks to a series of computers in China. Carpenter shared his discoveries with his military contacts, who passed the information to the FBI.

The FBI already knew about the attacks and had given them the code name "Titan Rain." However, it wasn't until Carpenter traced the cyberattacks to China that investigators realized they were

Titan Rain accessed networks belonging to the US Departments of State, Homeland Security, and Energy as well as UK defense and foreign ministries.

chasing the same group, rather than different individual hackers. The FBI recruited Carpenter to serve as an informant as he continued his pursuit of the hackers.

Despite Carpenter's and the FBI's work, they never caught the Titan Rain hackers. China also denied involvement, despite evidence that their government had backed the group. The Titan Rain attacks continued until 2007. During that time, hackers

THE TALLINN MANUAL

From 2009 to 2012, a group of legal experts met to develop guidelines on how international law relates to cyber warfare. The *Tallinn Manual on the International Law Applicable to Cyber Warfare*, later shortened to *Tallinn Manual*, referenced cyber espionage under Rule 32. The rule stated that cyber espionage was not technically legal or illegal. However, specific cases of cyber espionage might violate international espionage laws. Many individual countries, including the US, have laws prohibiting unauthorized access to computer systems.

Cambridge University Press published the *Tallinn Manual* in March 2013. It has become an invaluable resource for experts and advisors who deal with cyber issues.

infiltrated and stole confidential information from government agencies in the US and the United Kingdom. This included military plans, technical data, and government documents.

APT GROUPS

Titan Rain was the first known advanced persistent threat (APT) group. APT groups are organized groups of hackers who work on behalf of a government, military intelligence agency, or large corporation. APT groups work to steal government or military secrets or intellectual property. Sometimes, they also try to sabotage computer networks or influence political events, such as elections.

According to cybersecurity experts, there were more than 100 known APT groups in 2023. That number was expected to increase in the future.

The Titan Rain attacks alerted governments around the world to the fact that they were entering a dangerous new era of cyber espionage. Security experts realized that not only did government-sponsored hacking groups exist, but they could also be highly efficient and effective at stealing intelligence while avoiding detection. With the help of people such as Carpenter, the FBI and other security agencies began learning as much as they could about APTs and their tactics.

> **LONE WOLF HACKERS AND HACKTIVISTS**
>
> While most cyber espionage is the work of APT groups, individual hackers, known as lone wolf hackers, have been known to steal intelligence. Many lone wolf hackers break into government or military networks for no reason other than to see if they can. Others are known as hacktivists, and are motivated by a certain cause, such as publicizing a military's human rights violations.

ZERO-DAY ATTACKS

Titan Rain relied on many common cyber espionage techniques. But they were especially skilled at a tactic called zero-day attacks. A zero-day attack takes advantage of a security vulnerability in hardware or software before the manufacturer and developer are aware of it. It is known as a zero-day attack because the manufacturer and developer have zero days to fix the vulnerability.

In 2014, hackers used a zero-day attack to steal and publicly release Sony Pictures Entertainment's private corporate data, including the unreleased film Annie. Many believe the attack was in response to Sony's upcoming film The Interview.

Titan Rain used scanners to search thousands of computers for security vulnerabilities. These vulnerabilities allowed them to bypass built-in security measures, giving Titan Rain access to the computer's hard drive, where they could control the computer, download files, or even plant malware.

MALWARE 101

Malicious software, or malware, has been another favorite tool of cyber spies since the early days of cyber espionage. Malware is harmful software that is put onto a computer without the user's

« SPY HALL OF FAME »
THE EQUATION GROUP

The Equation Group is a powerful and sophisticated APT group that has been active since 2001. They are known for exploiting zero-day vulnerabilities to infect computer systems with malware. The malware reprograms an infected computer's hard drive and then self-destructs, making it untraceable. The Equation Group typically targets military, finance, and media outlets in countries that include Iran, Russia, and Afghanistan. The locations of these targets and the timing of the attacks have led many to suspect the group is tied to the US National Security Agency.

Equation Group attacks have affected at least 500 computer systems in 42 countries, though many experts believe the real number is much higher.

knowledge or consent. This software can damage the computer's processing ability, steal information, or make it easier for hackers to access the computer later. Titan Rain used malware to leave behind an undetectable beacon on each computer they accessed. The beacons worked like back doors, giving the hackers access to the computers even after the original vulnerability was patched, or fixed.

In 2013, a type of mass malware attack known as a watering hole attack targeted the US Department of Labor and Department of Energy websites. This is an attack where hackers hide malware on websites that their targets likely visit. In this case, it was sites used by government employees. When the employees visited the infected sites, the malware redirected them to a website that hosted spyware, which was automatically downloaded onto the users' computers.

Hackers redirected victims of the Department of Labor and Department of Energy attacks to a site hosting malware that monitored and stole their credentials and files.

DARKHOTEL AND PHISHING

Phishing is another tactic used by many APT groups. A phishing attack tricks somebody into providing sensitive information or downloading malware. Phishing attacks often use uninvited emails or text messages with links to websites or documents containing malware. The messages convince the user to launch a website, download malware, or respond with personal information, such as a social security number.

Some sophisticated phishing attacks, known as spear phishing attacks, are disguised as messages from a person or company the user trusts. DarkHotel is an APT group believed to be working on behalf of South Korea and is famous for its high-level spear phishing

DarkHotel targeted many luxury hotels in Macao, China, including the Wynn Palace hotel. These hotels were targets because they had plans to host international trade conferences.

SPORT PHISHING

In 2018, soccer fans around the world were getting ready for the biggest event in their sport, the World Cup. But in the months leading up to the first match, many soccer fans received unusual emails. Some emails stated the recipients had won a lottery and asked them to send their contact information to receive a cash prize. Other emails invited the recipients to register for a chance to win free event tickets. The emails seemed to be from FIFA, the organization that oversees international soccer competitions, including the World Cup. But the emails were actually part of a massive spear phishing campaign that gathered people's personal information. Experts aren't sure who was behind the attack. But similar attacks have since been launched surrounding other major sporting events, including the Olympic Games and the Super Bowl.

Leading up to the World Cup, hackers also sent emails with links to official-looking FIFA web pages and sites offering giveaways from partnering companies.

operations. The APT is called DarkHotel because it specifically targets travelers who connect to a hotel's wireless network (Wi-Fi). The APT group, which has been active since 2007, targets business executives and politicians.

DarkHotel hackers work by learning their targets' travel plans. Then, a few days before the target checks into their hotel, the APT group places malware on the hotel's server. Once the target connects to the hotel's Wi-Fi, they get a pop-up ad disguised to look like an update for a common program, such as Adobe. When the target downloads the "update," they actually install a piece of sophisticated spyware onto their device. As soon as the target checks out of the hotel, DarkHotel hackers remove the malware from the hotel's server, covering their tracks. Phishing and spear phishing are some of the most widely used cyber espionage campaigns. They are also important components of another popular cyber espionage technique called social engineering.

Online gambling and betting markets showed the odds of Trump being elected were lower on Russian holidays, when the trolls were less active.

CHAPTER 5

SOCIAL ENGINEERING AND CYBER SABOTAGE

In 2016, Russia's Internet Research Agency (IRA) began an ambitious campaign to influence US elections. The IRA had been meddling in US politics since 2014, but now it hoped to change the outcome of a US presidential election. The IRA's goal was to improve the election chances of Republican candidate Donald Trump. Russian leaders believed Trump would be a better ally than his opponent, Hillary Clinton.

ENTER THE TROLLS

In order to influence the election, the IRA hired "trolls" to create thousands of fake social media profiles and gain followers for each one. Trolls are people who intentionally post false information or offensive remarks online. The IRA's trolls posted controversial, divisive, and often misleading content to build support for Trump and decrease support for Clinton. The posts included lies about Clinton and controversial social issues to motivate certain Republican voters to vote for Trump. The trolls watched US TV shows and took English lessons to make their posts and online communications appear to come from Americans.

Many of the IRA trolls' profiles became highly influential, with one Facebook account having 1.8 million followers. The trolls were so effective that their actions were shown to influence polling.

THE WEAKEST LINK

Social engineering involves tricking people into performing an action or revealing information. The 2016 election trolls were part of one of the largest and most effective social engineering campaigns in history. Social engineering is also an important part of many cyber espionage techniques, including phishing and spear phishing. Most cybersecurity experts consider humans to be the weakest link in cybersecurity. Effective social engineering campaigns take advantage of human emotions, such as anger, excitement, fear, or even love.

The rise of social media has made social engineering easier than ever. In 2019, Pakistani spies set up fake social media profiles targeting Indian soldiers. The profiles featured pictures and bios of attractive women pretending to be interested in the soldiers. The soldiers unknowingly provided the spies with pictures of weaponry and other details about military operations. The operation worked

THE DEEP, DARK WEB

When you use your favorite search engine to look something up online, did you know that you are only accessing a small fraction of the internet? More than 90 percent of online content is part of the deep web. The deep web is made up of web pages that cannot be accessed by standard search engines, such as Google. Many of these websites require log-in credentials or otherwise restrict access. Others block search engine crawlers, which are bots that search the internet for content that can be indexed for search engines. Most information on the deep web is innocent, such as information on a school website that you need a username and password to access. However, about 5 percent of all internet content is on the dark web, which is part of the deep web. This content can only be accessed with a specialized browser, such as TOR. The dark web is not regulated by any country or company. As a result, it hosts a lot of illegal activity. Many cyber spies and terrorists use the dark web to communicate, plan, and execute their attacks.

TOR can also be used to protect a user's privacy online. It does this by encrypting internet traffic through its browser and deleting the cookies and browsing history after each session.

so well that India advised its soldiers to remove social media accounts from their phones and computers.

THE NATANZ MYSTERY

In January 2010, the International Atomic Energy Agency (IAEA) inspected the Natanz nuclear facility in Iran, a plant that used thousands of centrifuges to enrich uranium gas. The IAEA is a global organization dedicated to maintaining the safety and security of nuclear technology.

Natanz had a mysterious problem. The centrifuges, a vital part of the plant's operation, were failing at an alarming rate. The devices were supposed to last for ten years. But in the last few weeks, the plant's technicians had needed to replace them frequently. IAEA inspectors and Natanz technicians had no idea why.

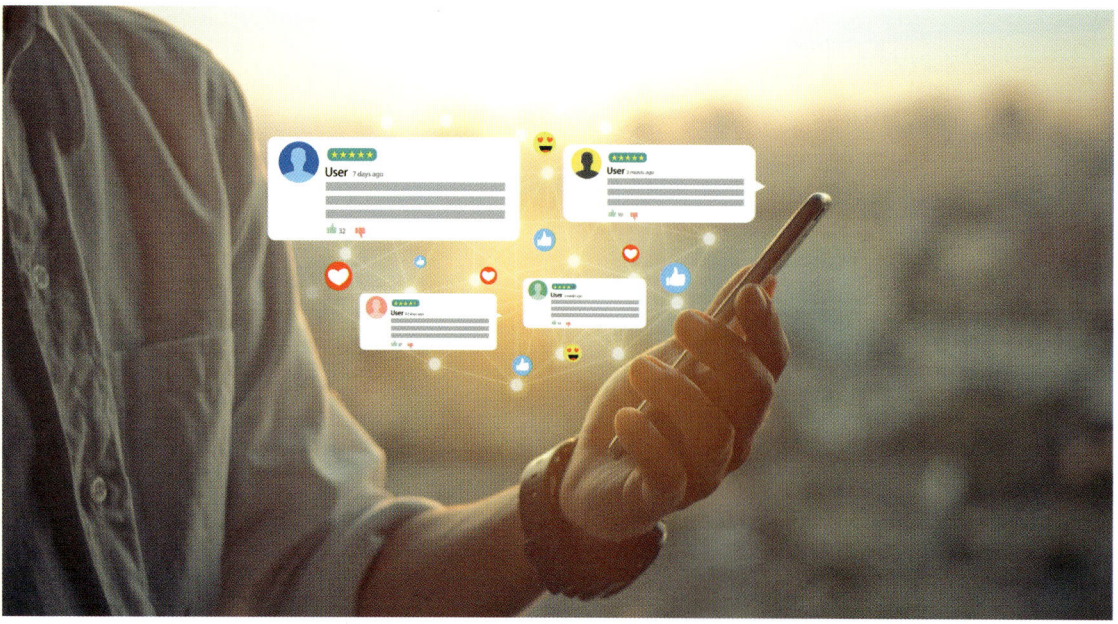

In 2023, a group of Ukrainian hackers also used social media to gain intelligence from Russian soldiers.

The IAEA was founded in 1957. Yukiya Amano was the director in January 2010 during the Natanz mystery.

Several months later, an Iranian engineering firm reported that its computers were acting strangely. The computers, even those newly updated, were mysteriously turning off and rebooting to a blue screen. The on-site security expert reached out to a cybersecurity firm in Belarus. Eventually, the firm tracked down the root of the problem, which had also caused Natanz's centrifuges to fail. It was a piece of malware known as Stuxnet.

STUXNET'S SECRETS

Stuxnet was like no malware that had come before. It didn't just steal information. It had the power to damage a computer's hardware, proving that cyber spies could now physically sabotage their rivals.

Stuxnet attacked the centrifuges at Natanz for more than a year. The malware increased the pressure inside the devices, damaging them and the uranium enrichment process.

Stuxnet targeted a computer's programmable logic controller (PLC) by using zero-day software. The PLC regulates a machine's electromechanical processes. Stuxnet had infiltrated the Natanz centrifuges' PLCs, causing them to malfunction. It also overrode any alerts used to warn Natanz's technicians of a problem.

Getting Stuxnet inside the Natanz plant was another espionage achievement. The Iranian nuclear plant was air gapped. This meant it had no computer network or internet connection for a hacker to exploit remotely. So, the hackers infected computers in companies

Stuxnet was able to infect more than 900 centrifuges at Natanz over a period of five months.

connected to Iran's nuclear program. When the companies transferred information to Natanz, they used USB drives. These drives now included Stuxnet, allowing the malware to spread to the highly secure nuclear plant.

Stuxnet was the first cyberweapon to cause widespread physical damage. Most experts believe Stuxnet was a collaboration between the US and Israeli security agencies to prevent Iran from developing nuclear weapons. Stuxnet surprised and alarmed intelligence agencies and governments around the world. Using cyber sabotage, hackers could damage machinery and even take down a system as vital as an electrical grid.

Many hackers working for other countries attack places such as FireEye so they can access the security firm's government and corporate clients.

CHAPTER 6

SPYING INTO THE FUTURE

SINCE 2013, CYBERSECURITY FIRM FIREEYE HAD BEEN the first responder to cyberattacks on Target Corporation, Sony Pictures Entertainment, and other high-profile clients. It had also been the go-to security firm for the US government. But in December 2020, FireEye announced that it had been hacked.

The attackers were believed to be a group of Russian cyber spies known as Cozy Bear. They used techniques FireEye had never seen before to access a highly secure digital vault that held its Red Team tools.

RED TEAM, BLUE TEAM

FireEye's Red Team was a group that used the tools and techniques of APT groups. It launched false cyberattacks on clients' websites. Meanwhile, FireEye's Blue Team mounted a defense. This process alerted FireEye's clients

« SPY HALL OF FAME »

FANCY BEAR AND COZY BEAR

Fancy Bear and Cozy Bear, believed to be backed by the Russian government, are two of the most infamous APT groups in the world. Fancy Bear has been active since 2008 and is thought to be part of the GRU, Russia's military intelligence agency. It's known for using zero-day exploits and spear phishing attacks to gather intelligence. Fancy Bear's top targets have been media companies, government agencies, and military organizations. In 2016, Fancy Bear hacked the Democratic National Committee, stealing user information and other intelligence.

Cozy Bear is Fancy Bear's more mysterious counterpart. It has been active since 2010 and is believed to operate on behalf of Russia's government intelligence agency, the FSB. Cozy Bear's main targets are the government institutions of Russia's rivals, including the US. The group is believed to work closely with Fancy Bear. But Cozy Bear operates with such secrecy that security experts can only guess which cyberattacks it is behind.

In 2015, Cozy Bear hacked the Pentagon, the headquarters of the US Department of Defense.

to any vulnerabilities while ensuring their websites and systems stayed secure from real hackers.

The Red Team's success depended on having the latest and greatest hacking tools. For years, they developed a collection of cyber tools that could breach websites. Now, Cozy Bear had access to all of them. FireEye was quick to report the breach to the FBI and publicly published a series of countermeasures. Anyone who was a victim from attacks using the stolen tools could use the countermeasures to protect themselves.

The 2020 FireEye attack proved what most cybersecurity experts already suspected. The world of cyber espionage was changing faster than ever before. Cyber spies were constantly developing new and innovative techniques to hack into systems. Emerging technologies, such as artificial intelligence (AI), also provided new opportunities for cyber spies to launch sophisticated cyberattacks.

AI AND NLP

AI is the capability of a computer to learn and think in a way that mimics human intelligence. The technology has been in use since the 1980s, but it grew in popularity in the 2020s.

Virtual assistants such as Apple's Siri rely on NLP to respond to users' questions.

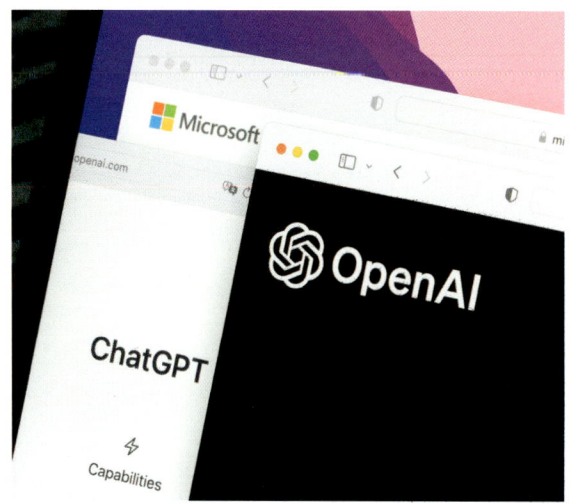

ChatGPT is an AI chatbot created by OpenAI in 2022. It is mostly used to hold text conversations, but it can also write computer code, mimic different writing styles, and more.

In 2023, about 80 percent of Americans owned a smartphone.

Advancements such as natural language processing (NLP) made AI more powerful than ever before. NLP helps computers use AI to generate spoken and written language the same way a human would. Cyber spies can use NLP to generate convincing spear phishing emails that are incredibly hard to identify as fake.

AI can also automatically scan websites and networks to look for vulnerabilities. It can crack passwords and design smart malware that learns and adapts to avoid cybersecurity tools. Hackers can even use AI data mining to improve the success of a social engineering campaign. Data mining involves using AI to analyze enormous amounts of online data, looking for patterns and trends and identifying potential targets. The AI can then generate images and social media posts based on its analysis.

A DIGITAL PLAYBOOK

AI is a powerful tool, but one of the greatest opportunities for cyber spies might be sitting in your pocket or backpack. Nearly 7 billion people in the world carry smartphones. These devices contain information about a user's name, location, contacts, communication, and even personality. Smartphones can operate almost like a digital playbook or guide, telling a spy everything they need to know about a target.

Cyber spies have found ways to easily access all the data on a target's

INTERNET OF THINGS

The internet of things (IoT) is the system of interconnected digital devices that communicate with one another using the internet. This includes smart devices, such as your digital assistant, smartphone, or TV. But as technology improves, formerly "dumb" devices such as refrigerators, toasters, and thermometers are joining the IoT. The online communication of devices helps machines operate more efficiently, making daily life easier. But the IoT also opens a whole new world for cyber spies. IoT devices are constantly gathering information and uploading it to the cloud. If hacked, all this information can be downloaded directly into the hands of cyber spies.

Cybersecurity firms can protect their clients by using the same technologies cyber spies use.

smartphone using a tool called an IMSI catcher. IMSI catchers are fake cell phone towers. They are hidden in public places such as airports. An IMSI catcher intercepts a phone's signal before it can connect to a cell tower. The catcher can then extract data from the phone, including text messages, emails, or even websites the user visited. IMSI detectors can even install malware on a device, allowing the spies to continue tracking the phone after it has left the area.

A DIGITAL FUTURE

Digital technologies are changing faster than ever before. The rise in quantum computing may lead to computers that are more than 100 million times faster than standard computers. Cyber spies

BECOMING A CYBER CRIME FIGHTER

Getting a job at the FBI is a sure way to find yourself on the front lines of the war against cyber espionage. To become a member of the FBI's cyber crime squad, you must be a US citizen with a college degree and have strong computer skills. Aspiring agents need to complete a lengthy application process, pass a background check, and pass medical and fitness requirements before beginning a rigorous training program.

could one day use these computers in their attacks. Virtual reality technology has also created new opportunities for cyber spies to connect with their targets. And predictive analytics has allowed cybersecurity teams to improve their defenses against possible attacks.

The world of cyber espionage may be changing quickly. But talented security experts around the world are working hard to stop cyber espionage before it starts, protect data, and make the world a safer place.

SO YOU WANT TO BE A CYBER DEFENDER?

Cyber spies can be anywhere and everywhere. Anytime you log on to public Wi-Fi, visit a new website, or download a new app, you could be allowing a spy to steal your information! The best way to beat a cyber spy at their own game is to practice cyber hygiene. These practices can help you stay safe and protect your information online. Do you have what it takes to master the art of cybersecurity? Complete the missions below to find out.

MISSION 1
KNOW YOUR NETWORKS

Public Wi-Fi networks are one of the greatest risks to cybersecurity. These free networks, such as those provided by airports, malls, or coffee shops, can be accessed by anyone, including hackers. Protect your security by limiting your use of public Wi-Fi networks. If you do use public Wi-Fi, make sure any websites you visit are encrypted. This means the website scrambles data into a code. Look for a lock symbol next to the URL in your web browser to know if a website is encrypted.

MISSION 2
DO A CYBER SPRING CLEANING

First, install any available software updates for your devices' operating systems. Then, review all the apps and programs downloaded on your devices, including

your phone, tablet, and computer. Uninstall any apps or programs that you no longer use. If you have multiple applications serving the same function, choose one to keep and delete the others. Then update all your remaining apps. Change passwords and enable two-factor authentication if it's an option. Next, review the privacy settings for each app and turn off any unnecessary permissions the app doesn't need to function, such as location or Bluetooth.

MISSION 3
CHECK YOUR COOKIES

Most websites use cookies to improve functionality and collect information. These are small text files that help websites remember user information, such as items in a digital shopping cart or login credentials. But hackers can use cookies to steal your information. You can control how a website uses cookies through your browser's settings. You can choose to enable all cookies or just necessary cookies that improve the site's functionality.

MISSION 4
BE SMART WITH YOUR SOCIAL MEDIA

When you post something online, it's there forever. Make sure any content you post isn't something you wouldn't want your family or a future boss to see. Be aware of what clues about yourself could be hidden in a posted picture, such as where you live or go to school. Be careful about which people you accept as friends online. Try to limit them to people you know in real life to avoid fake profiles.

TIMELINE

French king Louis XIV forms a *cabinet noir* to intercept and read private letters.
LATE 1600s

The American Civil War
1861–1865

Guglielmo Marconi invents wireless radio technology.
1894

Computer networks adopt the Transfer Control Protocol/Internetwork Protocol, the first standard protocol for internet communication.
1983

1837
Samuel F.B. Morse invents the telegraph, the first form of electronic communication.

1947–1991
The Cold War

1939–1945
World War II

1914–1918
World War I

1969
The DOD uses ARPANET to deliver the first successful internet message.

1988
Robert Tappan Morris launches the Morris Worm.

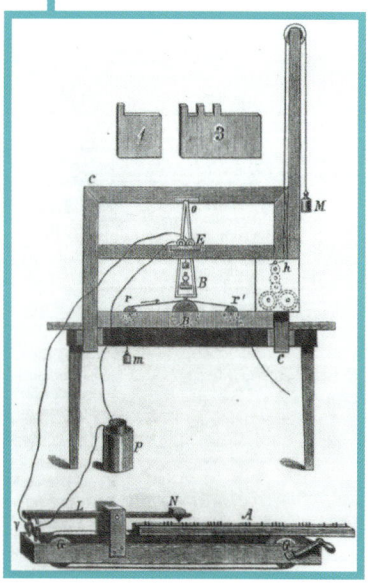

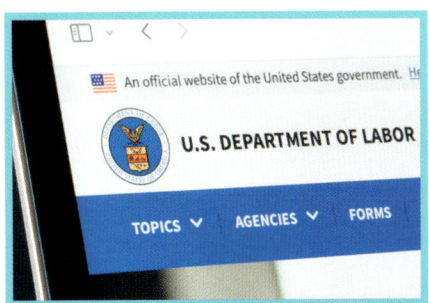

Tim Berners-Lee founds the World Wide Web.
1989

DarkHotel begins targeting business executives and politicians by hacking into luxury hotel Wi-Fi networks.
2007

The US Department of Labor and Department of Energy websites are targeted in a massive watering hole attack.
2013

2006
Julian Assange founds WikiLeaks.

2003–2007
A Chinese APT group launches the Titan Rain cyberattacks.

2010
The Stuxnet virus infects centrifuges at Iran's Natanz nuclear plant.

2018
Hackers target World Cup fans in a phishing campaign.

2020
Russian APT Cozy Bear hacks cybersecurity firm FireEye.

GLOSSARY

activist—a person who takes direct action in support of or in opposition to an issue.

analyst—a person who determines the meaning of something by breaking down its parts.

asylum—the protection given by a nation to someone who feels unsafe returning to his or her country.

beacon—a signal used for guidance.

centrifuge—a machine that separates substances by spinning.

civilian—a person who is not an active member of the military.

Civil War—the war between the United States of America and the Confederate States of America from 1861 to 1865.

classified—kept from the public in order to protect national security.

divisive—creating disagreement and anger.

encrypt—to convert information or data into a cipher or code to prevent unauthorized access.

espionage—the secret gathering of information on others.

hacker—a person who illegally accesses a computer system.

infiltrate—to enter a place secretly and without permission.

intercept—to interrupt something on its way from one place to another.

NASA—National Aeronautics and Space Administration. NASA is a US government agency that manages the nation's space program and conducts flight research.

potential—having the ability to occur or be achieved in the future.

protocol—a set of rules governing the data in a communications system.

quantum computing—using computers that make use of the quantum states of subatomic particles to store information.

sabotage—to harm an enemy nation's defenses by damaging or destroying something on purpose.

vulnerability—a weakness in a system's design.

ONLINE RESOURCES

To learn more about cyber spying, please visit **abdobooklinks.com** or scan this QR code. These links are routinely monitored and updated to provide the most current information available.

INDEX

A
advanced persistent threat (APT), 31-39, 41, 51-53
ARPANET, 18-20
Art of War, The, 11-12
artificial intelligence (AI), 53-55
Assange, Julian, 7-9

B
Berners-Lee, Tim, 21
Blue Team, 51
botnet, 28-29

C
cabinet noir, 12
Carpenter, Shawn, 31-33, 35
centrifuge, 46-48
Civil War, 13, 15
Clinton, Hillary, 9, 43-44
Cold War, 16, 18
Computer Fraud and Abuse Act, 24
computer virus, 24-25, 27
computer worm, 24-25
Confederate, 15
Cozy Bear, 51-53

D
dark web, 45
DarkHotel, 38-39, 41
data mining, 54-55
deep web, 45
Democratic National Committee (DNC), 9, 52
Department of Defense (DOD), 18
Department of Energy, 38
Department of Justice, 9
Department of Labor, 38

E
elections, 9, 34, 43-44
Electronic Numerical Integrator and Computer (ENIAC), 17
Equation Group, 37
Espionage Act, 9

F
Fancy Bear, 52
Federal Bureau of Investigation (FBI), 27, 32-33, 35, 53, 57
FireEye, 51, 53
FSB, 52

G
GRU, 52

I
IMSI catcher, 56
International Atomic Energy Agency (IAEA), 46
internet of things (IoT), 55
Internet Research Agency (IRA), 43-44
internet service provider (ISP), 6, 21

K
keylogger, 28

L
Lincoln, Abraham, 13
Louis XIV, 12

M
malware, 28-29, 36-41, 47-49, 54, 56
Manning, Bradley (Chelsea), 6, 8-9
Marconi, Guglielmo, 16
Massachusetts Institute of Technology (MIT), 23-24
Morris, Robert Tappan, 24-25
Morris Worm, 23-26
Morse, Samuel F.B., 13

N
Natanz nuclear facility, 46-49
National Security Agency, 37
natural language processing (NLP), 53-54
New York Times, 24-25

O
Obama, Barack, 5
Onion Router, the (TOR), 6, 45

P
phishing, 38-41, 44, 46, 52, 54
predictive analytics, 57
programmable logic controller (PLC), 48

R
ransomware, 29
Red Team, 51, 53

S
Sanders, Bernie, 9
Sandia National Laboratories, 31
smartphone, 55-56
Smith, Khan, 29
social engineering, 41, 43-44, 46, 54
social media, 43-44, 46, 55
software, 28-29, 35-39, 48-49
Sony Pictures Entertainment, 36, 51
spear phishing, 39-41, 44, 52, 54
spyware, 29, 38, 41
Stanton, Edwin, 15
Stuxnet, 47-49

T
Tallinn Manual, 33
Target Corporation, 51
telegraph, 13, 15-16
threat actors, 27, 31-41
Titan Rain, 32-36, 38
Transfer Control Protocol/Internetwork Protocol, 20
Trojan horse, 28
troll, 43-44
Trump, Donald, 9, 43-44
Tzu, Sun, 11

U
Union, 13, 15
Union of Soviet Socialist Republics (USSR), 16

V
virtual reality, 57

W
WikiLeaks, 5-9, 11
wireless network (Wi-Fi), 41
World War I, 9, 15-16
World War II, 16-17
World Wide Web (WWW), 21

Z
zero-day attack, 35-37, 48, 52